Stitches in Rhyme

Mother Goose Embroidered Quilts (and More!)

for the Modern Nursery

By Donna di Natale and Amy Ubben

Stitches in Rhyme

Mother Goose Embroidered Quilts (and More!)
for the Modern Nursery

By Donna di Natale and Amy Ubben

Editor: **Deb Rowden**

Designer: **Kim Walsh**

Photography: **Aaron T. Leimkuehler**

Illustration: **Eric Sears**

Technical Editor: **Andrea Uustalu**

Photo Editor: **Jo Ann Groves**

Published by:
Kansas City Star Books
1729 Grand Blvd.
Kansas City, Missouri, USA 64108

First edition, first printing
ISBN: 978-1-61169-130-6

Library of Congress Control Number: 2014939097

Printed in the United States of America by Walsworth Publishing Co., Marceline, MO

To order copies, call StarInfo at (816) 234-4473.

KANSAS CITY STAR
QUILTS
Continuing the Tradition

KansasCityStarQuilts.com

Acknowledgements

Thank you. Merci. Gracias. Danke. Grazie. No matter how you say it, a simple thank you never seems to be enough. Like celebrities accepting an Oscar, one is always afraid they will miss someone who needs to be thanked. And then there are those who go a bit too far, such as Steven Spielberg when he thanked his parents for not using birth control.

Anyway, our deepest gratitude to:

Our families, first and foremost, for allowing us to indulge in our passion for quilting.

Sally Bartos, daughter of LaVerne and Stanley Bartos, for sharing her mother's story. I really should thank Mark Zuckerberg for creating Facebook. I'll never forget that fateful day when I decided to search for "Sally Bartos" on Facebook, and there you were. I'm hoping your mother would approve of this book.

Freda Smith, for insisting that an overall pattern was perfect for the Nursery Rhyme quilt. You were absolutely right, and your quilting, as always, is beautiful!

Jackie Rudolph, for making a batch of Humpty Dumpty dolls and for proving that you really can't make just one.

Doug and Megan Ubben, for allowing us to photograph the projects in their beautiful home.

And last, but certainly not least, to our super team at Kansas City Star Quilts: Doug, Deb R., Eric, Kim, Aaron, Jo Ann, Edie, Diane, Andrea, Deb B. and Jack. You are the best!

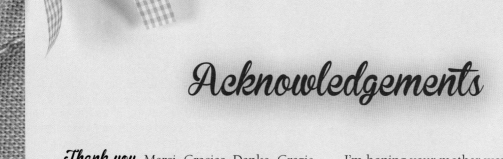

SING A SONG OF SIXPENCE

Donna di Natale

This is Donna's third book for Kansas City Star Quilts. When working on her second book, "Prized Quilts," she discovered the Nursery Rhyme series published in the Omaha (Nebraska) World-Herald and fell in love with it. There wasn't room for all the blocks in that book, so book three was born. Not having any grandchildren of her own, Donna turned to her good friend Amy Ubben for help and inspiration.

Like Amy, Donna loves both quilting and embroidery. Donna has been sewing since age 5, when she made her first doll quilt, embroidered with Raggedy Ann and Andy. With the embroidered projects in this book, she has come full circle.

Donna lives in Lenexa, Kansas, and quilts with two cats. Murphy thinks he has to inspect and approve every single project Donna makes, while Zoey plays the princess and wonders when Donna will stop sewing and fix dinner.

Amy Ubben

Amy has been sewing since she took a sampler quilting class as a teenager, back in the days when quilting was done by hand. She hand-pieced an entire full-size quilt top in a terrible green color. She promptly stuck it in a bag and never looked at it again.

Fast-forward 25 years – now she has mountains of beautiful fabric to choose from. Amy has machine-quilted projects ranging from table runners to queen-size quilts. She loves visiting with friends while doing embroidery work.

This book is a great opportunity to combine her love of quilting, embroidery, and babies. She designed the projects with her own grandchildren in mind, remembering that when her daughter Erica was born, an aunt gave her a small handmade quilt that Erica still cherishes 30 years later.

Table of Contents

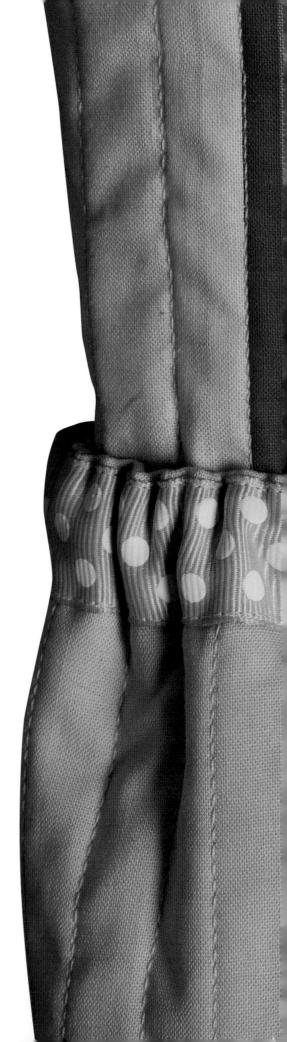

Introduction

Who Was LaVerne Bartos?

In September of 1940, the first of 21 embroidered quilt blocks simply called the Nursery Rhyme series was published in the Omaha (Nebraska) World-Herald. The blocks, based on beloved Mother Goose rhymes, became one of the most popular series the World-Herald ever printed. A February 24, 1941, World-Herald article reported 1,000 orders for reprints had been received from readers in 13 states.

The embroidery designs were created by LaVerne Bartos, a name not often heard in the quilting world. So who was LaVerne Bartos?

LaVerne was born in 1914 to John and Christina Brauer of Crete, Nebraska. When LaVerne was 4 years old, her sister Marjorie was born. Excited about her new baby sister, LaVerne started drawing pictures of babies and long-legged storks, bassinets and toys, everything a baby would enjoy. The drawings were made in an old bank ledger her mother gave her. As Marjorie grew older, the girls began working together, spending many happy hours with their pencils and paints – LaVerne doing the drawing, and Marjorie the coloring.

LaVerne continued drawing in school and became quite popular with other children who asked her to make special drawings for them. When LaVerne was 10, her mother bought her a blackboard and colored chalk. The company that manufactured the chalk had a contest that year to see which child could make the best drawing using their chalk. LaVerne drew a blacksmith's shop, with the smithy shoeing a horse in front of the shop, and won the $5 first prize.

In high school, LaVerne used her drawing skills to create posters for various school events and cartoons for the school newspaper. To make her own spending money, she drew and sold placecards, party favors, and silhouettes painted on glass. When she began drawing paper dolls, so many children would beg for them that her mother instructed her to charge a nickel for every doll, thinking it would reduce the crowds of children in the house. It made no difference. The children continued to come, bringing their nickels.

In the mid-1930s, LaVerne married Stanley Bartos, from nearby Wilber, Nebraska. They had two daughters, Suzanne and Sally, and a son, Stanley Jr. LaVerne soon began drawing for the Omaha World-Herald. The drawings appeared on "Aunt Clara's Page," a section devoted to "stories, games and puzzles for boy and girl readers." According to LaVerne's daughter Sally, "Aunt Clara" actually was LaVerne's aunt. LaVerne contributed drawings for coloring contests. Pictured here is a drawing from October 8, 1939. The children and dog are reminiscent of those that would later appear in the nursery rhyme blocks.

LaVerne continued to draw paper dolls and submit them to the World-Herald. One of her first dolls was Jean, a sweet little girl with a party dress and doll, whom she admitted was modeled after her daughter, Suzanne.

She drew a wide variety of dolls, from children to adults, with clothes that ranged from historical to the latest fashions. She even drew a Sonja doll, based on world-champion figure skater Sonja Henie.

Coloring Contest
Since Sonja Henie has come to Nebraska, LaVerne Bartos thought you would enjoy having her as a paper doll. Color her to the best of your ability and send her and her clothes back to Aunt Clara. Both over and under "11" will receive a prize for the best work.

for the Modern Nursery

LaVerne Bartos and Her Daughter, Suzanne

to stay indoors at recess to draw for them. All the seats near hers would be crowded with little girls urging her to draw in their

Fishing Garb in Alaska

ALASKA

Typical fur costume in Alaska.

LaVerne's paper dolls were so popular that she became known as the "Paper Doll Lady." A photograph of LaVerne and Suzanne appeared in the newspaper on July 30, 1939, revealing to her many fans the "real" paper doll lady.

In 1939, LaVerne drew her first series of quilt blocks, the nursery rhyme blocks reproduced in this book. A second series of 20 embroidered quilt blocks, Costumes of the Nationalities, began appearing on October 1, 1941. Consisting of a boy or girl wearing a national costume, the blocks included England, Sweden, Scotland, Hawaii, Egypt, Portugal, Turkey, Spain, India, Alaska, Japan, Poland, Italy, Mexico, Arabia, Czechoslovakia, Holland, Indian (representing Native Americans), China, and the United States. This series ran through January 24, 1942.

During World War II, LaVerne and Stanley lived in Arizona, where he served at Camp Florence, the largest prisoner of war complex in the United States. Set in the middle of the desert, it housed thousands of Italian and German prisoners taken during the North African campaign.

After the war, Stanley and LaVerne returned to Nebraska farm life and LaVerne again picked up her pen, this time writing a column called "Country Style," and using "A Farm Woman" as her byline. The columns told of post-war life on a Midwest farm and were illustrated with her drawings of farm animals and/or children. The children, Tony and Sarah, were pseudonyms for her own small children.

When Stanley took a job with the Bureau of Indian Affairs, the family moved from Nebraska to Colorado, then to Arizona again, where they lived on the Navajo reservation. There, LaVerne was employed by the Navajo Tribal Utility Authority. One of her responsibilities was to design and illustrate booklets to educate the residents on the new electrical service. LaVerne created a character named Kee Kilowatt to demonstrate the various advantages of electricity and the safe use of appliances such as washing machines, refrigerators, irons, and sewing machines. Kee, a common Navajo name, was very much like Reddy Kilowatt, a character introduced in 1926 by the Alabama Power Company. Kee was distinctly Navajo, however, sporting a feather in his headband.

LaVerne continued to enjoy drawing and passed the talent on to her daughters. While living on the reservation, she created coloring books for the schoolchildren. Sally fondly recalls making one of these coloring books with her mother and how much the children enjoyed receiving the books. Sally went on to be a professional artist. She now resides in New Mexico, and her paintings reflect the scenes and bright colors of the region.

Although LaVerne Bartos left us with only two quilt block series, it is our resolve that she and her talent will not be lost to time. Enjoy the patterns reproduced here, and remember the lovely woman who designed them for generations to come.

General Instructions

Here are a few general rules that apply to all these projects.

All yardage is based on 42-44″ wide fabric.

1/4″ seams are used throughout, unless otherwise noted.

Always use **the highest quality** 100% cotton fabric that you can afford. The difference is amazing. The fabrics are easier to work with and will last much longer. Consider that you are making a keepsake that will be treasured for years to come. That said, use light to medium weight fabric for the embroidered pieces. We used Bella solids by Moda for all of the solid fabrics.

Always, always **include a label** on the quilt. The simplest label we know of is a rectangle of fabric stitched to the back of the quilt with your name and date written on it in permanent ink. Other information to include could be the recipient's name, the date given, the occasion, and the location. All information will be greatly appreciated in the future. For a sample label, see page 65.

Embroidery Instructions

Always check to make sure your embroidery floss is colorfast. A small piece soaked in warm water and dried on a white paper towel will confirm that. Red floss is especially tricky. We used DMC floss for all our embroidery.

Because the designs are embroidered on white or light fabric, always **wash your hands** before picking up needle and thread. Try to keep the pets off of the blocks. (I know this is especially difficult with cats.)

If you find your stitches becoming longer or more uneven, stop and **take a break.** It is difficult to maintain small, even stitches when you are tired.

The instructions suggest that you use **interfacing** behind your embroidery. This hides your stitches and provides support for the design. We used woven fusible interfacing (Pellon SF101 Shape-Flex), but you may want to use nonwoven interfacing or muslin. Use whatever works best for you.

Follow the Illustrations on the next page for the **embroidery stitches** used. Feel free to try other stitches to obtain the look you want.

The same goes for **floss color.** The decision to use one color or multiple colors is entirely up to you. If you color the design with crayons we recommend using floss to match the colors or black floss to contrast.

A fun and simple way to enhance embroidery is to color in the designs using Crayola brand crayons. This should be done <u>before</u> adding the embroidery stitches. After coloring the design, lay a paper towel over the block and press with a hot, dry iron to melt the wax and set the color. Add more color or shading as desired. Crayons were used to enhance the Jack and Jill block on the Magic Changing Pad (page 38).

Tracing the Designs
Begin by folding the fabric square in half and in half again, forming a smaller square. Lightly press and open.

Trace the embroidery design onto the right side of the fabric, using the creases to center and straighten the design. The box around the design is only for ease in tracing – don't trace it onto the fabric.

There are many methods for **tracing designs onto fabric.**
- Erasable or removable pen or pencil. Be sure to test the pen or pencil on a piece of the fabric you will be using to make sure the marks will disappear or wash away.
- Micron pen. The ink is permanent but if you use a 0.5 pen, it makes a 0.45 mm line that will usually be covered up by the embroidery.

A **light box** or light table is handy for tracing, but a sunny window will work just as well. Tape both the pattern and the fabric to the surface so they won't slip or slide.

Another option for embroidering the designs is use of a wash-away stabilizer, such as Transfer-Eze. Photocopy the design onto the transfer medium and adhere it to the right side of the fabric. After the embroidery is completed, trim the stabilizer and immerse it in water until the stabilizer dissolves.

After the design is traced onto the fabric, fuse the interfacing to the reverse side of each square. If you are using non-fusible interfacing or muslin, simply layer the fabrics.

Place the square in an embroidery hoop and embroider the design. We used 2 strands of floss for the main design and 1 strand for small details.

Press the block on the reverse side. Square and trim the block to the size stated in the pattern.

When sewing embroidered blocks together, always check to make sure that the embroidery is right side up.

French Knot

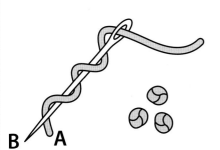

Stem Stitch

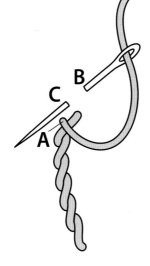

Chain Stitch

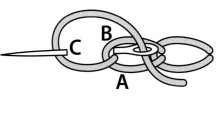

Running Stitch

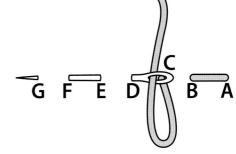

Lazy Daisy Stitch

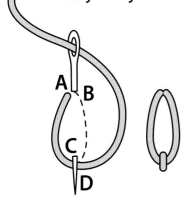

Split Stitch

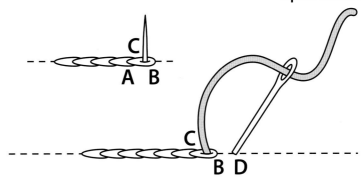

Floss colors used in these projects:

- DMC 809 Delft blue (quilt, pillow, curtains)
- DMC 321 red
- DMC 312 very dark baby blue (carrier cover)
- DMC 704 bright chartreuse: (diaper bag)
- DMC 310 black
- DMC 743 medium yellow
- DMC 869 very dark hazelnut brown
- DMC 3828 hazelnut brown
- DMC 740 tangerine (flowers)
- DMC 3770 very light tawny (flesh)
- DMC 702 kelly green

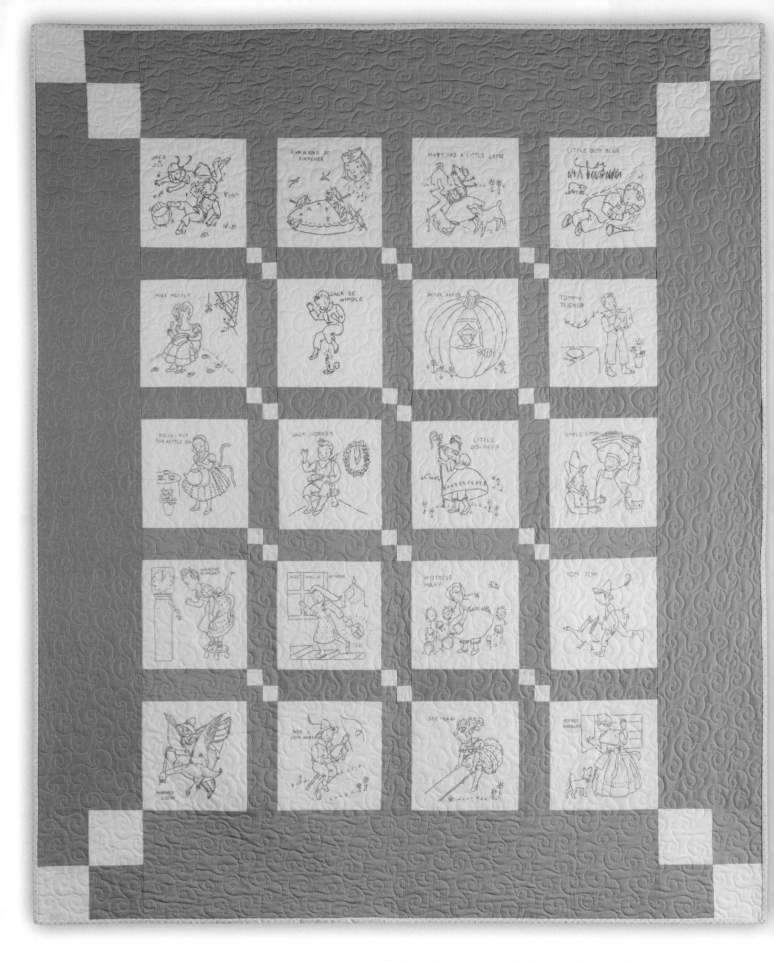

Designed by Donna • Embroidered and pieced by Amy • Quilted by Freda Smith

Finished quilt size: 45″ x 57″ • Finished block size: 7″ x 7″

Nursery Rhyme Quilt

The original published layout for the Nursery Rhyme quilt included all 21 embroidered blocks plus 21 solid blocks, for a finished size of 56″ x 63″. We deleted the solid blocks and added sashing to make this quilt the perfect size for today's cribs or toddler beds. To balance the number of blocks, poor Humpty Dumpty fell off of the quilt, only to reappear later.

Fabric and Supplies
Blue: 1 1/3 yards
(1 1/2 yards if making quilt and pillow, page 24)
White: 1 3/4 yards (if making all 21 squares)
Woven fusible interfacing: 2 3/4 yards
Backing: 3 yards
Batting: twin size
Binding: 1/2 yard
Embroidery floss: DMC 809

Cutting Instructions
Blue
2 – 7 1/2″ x 43 1/2″ (side borders)
2 – 7 1/2″ x 34 1/2″ (top borders)
2 – 7 1/2″ x width of fabric (WOF);
sub-cut into 31 – 2 1/2″ x 7 1/2″ rectangles (sashing)
1 – 4″ x WOF; sub-cut into 8 – 4″ squares
1 – 1 1/2″ x WOF (cornerstones)

White
20 – 9″ x 9″ (trim to 7 1/2″ x 7 1/2″ after embroidered)
1 – 4″ x WOF; sub-cut into 8 – 4″ squares (cornerstones)
1 – 1 1/2″ x WOF

Interfacing
20 – 9″ x 9″ squares

Embroidery Instructions
Embroider the blocks following the Embroidery Instructions (page 14). There are 21 embroidery designs (patterns are on pages 69-89). You will use 20 for the quilt top and 1 for the back. Humpty Dumpty fell to the back of our quilt. Who will you put on the back of yours?

Sashing

Sewing Instructions

1. Sew the blue 1 1/2" x WOF strip to the white 1 1/2" x WOF strip.

2. Sub-cut into 24 – 1 1/2" pieces.

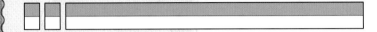

3. Sew 2 pieces together, reversing one piece, to form the checkered cornerstones. Make 12 cornerstone squares.

4. Sew 4 sashing rectangles 2 1/2" x 7 1/2" and 3 cornerstones into a sashing strip. Make 4.

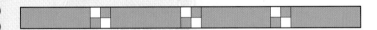

5. Lay out your embroidered squares according to the Assembly Diagram on page 19. Beginning with the top row, sew blocks and the remaining 2 1/2" x 7 1/2" sashing pieces into rows.

6. Sew a sashing strip to the bottom of each row.

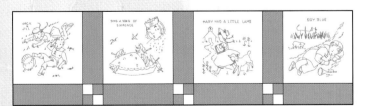

Borders

Side

1. Sew a side border (7 1/2" x 43 1/2") strip to both sides of the quilt top.

Top/Bottom

1. Sew a 4" x WOF blue strip to the 4" x WOF white strip to make a strip set.

2. Sub-cut into 8 – 4" blue/white pieces.

3. Sew 2 blue/white pieces together, reversing one piece, to make a checkered corner block. Make 4.

4. Sew a corner block to each end of the top and bottom border (7 1/2" x 34 1/2") strips.

5. Sew the top and bottom borders to the quilt top.

6. Quilt and bind.

Note: Freda recommended an overall meander quilting design (even in the embroidered blocks) and this worked beautifully.

Assembly Diagram

Nursery Rhyme Curtain

Finished curtain panel: 23 1/2″ x 32″ • Finished embroidered block size: 7″ x 7″

Designed and made by Amy

Matching curtain panels add so much to a room. Choose your favorite block or two to coordinate with the Nursery Rhyme Quilt. While the quilt uses 4-patch cornerstones, the curtains use 9-patch corners - either will work for both the quilt and the curtains.

Fabric and Supplies

Before you begin, measure your window length and width. There are 2 panels. Each panel width should be approximately the width of the window so there is fullness in the curtains as they hang. The length of the curtains depends on whether you want to hang them from the top of the window frame or some-where mid-way down the frame - you will need to measure and cut accordingly.

Note: The yardage and measurements given here are for a standard 32″ x 66″ window.

Blue: 1/4 yard

White: 3 1/4 yards

Embroidery floss: DMC 809

Fusible interfacing : 1 yard (20″ wide)

Batting: 1 piece approximately 18" x 25" (see Cutting Instructions)

Ribbon: 6 1/2 yards of 1 5/16″ wide ribbon for hanging curtains

Cutting Instructions

Blue

2 - 2 3/4″ x 22″ (cornerstones)
1 - 2 3/4″ x 11″ (cornerstones)

White

2 - 2 3/4″ x 11″ (cornerstones)
1 - 2 3/4″ x 22″ (cornerstones)
2 - 9″ x 15″ (center embroidered piece)
2 - 24 1/2″ x 26″ for front upper curtain panel
2 - 24 1/2″ x 33″ for back curtain panel

Batting

Cut a piece to fit the back of the strip containing the 9-patch corners plus the center embroidered square. That piece should be cut into 2 pieces, each 9″ x 25″. This left a little extra to trim off after quilting.

Interfacing or stabilizer: 2 – 9″ x 15″

Ribbon: 14 – 16″ strips (7 per panel)

Make the Center Block

Embroider the block of your choice following the Embroidery Instructions (page 14).
Press on the reverse side. Trim to 7 1/2" tall x 12" wide. For these curtain panels, the corners are square, but the embroidered section is a rectangle.

9-Patch Corners

Sewing Instructions

1. Sew a blue 2 3/4" x 22" strip to the top and bottom of a white 2 3/4" x 22" strip, so that you have 3 rows (blue/white/blue).

2. Sub-cut into 8 – 2 3/4" strips.

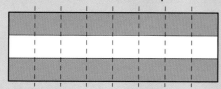

3. Sew a white 2 3/4" X 11" strip to the top and bottom of a blue 2 3/4" x 11" strip, making 3 rows (white/blue/white).

4. Sub-cut into 4 – 2 3/4" strips.

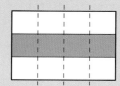

5. Sew the strips together forming 4 – 9-patch blocks (2 for each curtain panel).

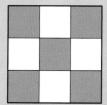

Assembly

1. Sew the corner squares to the embroidered center rectangle. Adjust the width of the panel some by trimming the center rectangle. Press. This forms the bottom front of the curtain panel.

2. Baste the batting piece to the back of the bottom curtain panel. Quilt as desired. After quilting, trim it to 7 1/2" x 24 1/2".

3. Stitch a white 24 1/2" x 26" rectangle to the top of the quilted bottom piece along the 24 1/2" edge.

4. Pin the 24 1/2" x 33" back panel to the front panel, right sides together. Stitch the bottom and sides of panel. Turn it right side out like a pillowcase. Fold the top edges 1/2" toward the inside. Press. Fold each 16" piece of ribbon in half, and pin along the top edge about 2 1/4" apart (7 on each panel depending on the width of your ribbon), starting and ending at an edge. Stitch along the top edge to close the panel and secure ribbon.

Stitches in Rhyme

Sleepyhead Pillow Cover

Finished size: 12″ x 12″
Designed and made by Donna

Use this pillow cover to store the quilt when it is not in use, or fill it with a 12″ x 12″ pillow form.
The envelope-style closure on the back means no zippers or buttonholes are required.

Fabric and Supplies

Blue: 1 fat quarter or 1/4 yard

White: 1 fat quarter for embroidered block and cornerstones

Polka dot: 1/2 yard for back

Fusible interfacing: 1/3 yard

Pillow insert: 16" x 16"

Embroidery floss: DMC 809

Cutting Instructions

White
1 – 9 1/2" x 9 1/2" square for embroidery
1 – 2 1/2" x 22" strip (cornerstones)

Blue
4 – 4 1/2" x 8 1/2" rectangles
1 – 2 1/2" x 22" strip (cornerstones)

Polka Dot
2 – 12 1/2" x 16 1/2" rectangles

Interfacing: 1 – 9 1/2" square

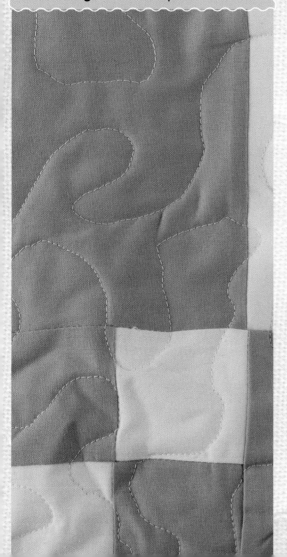

Make the Center Block

Embroider the block of your choice following the Embroidery Instructions on page 14. Press on the reverse side. Trim to 8 1/2" square.

Make the Pillow Front

1. Sew the 2 1/2" x 22" white strip to the 2 1/2" x 22" blue strip to make a white/blue strip set.

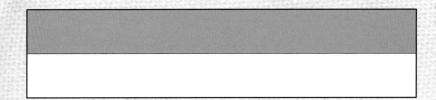

2. Sub-cut into 8 – 2 1/2" pieces.

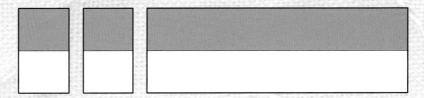

3. Sew 2 pieces together, reversing one piece, to form the cornerstones. Make 4 cornerstone squares.

4. Sew one 8 1/2" blue strip to each side of the white square.

5. Sew one cornerstone to each end of the remaining 8 1/2" blue strips. Sew one to the top and one to the bottom.

BOY BLUE

Your pillow front should measure 12 1/2" square.

Make the Back

1. Fold one long edge (16 1/2") of each of the 12 1/2" x 16 1/2" polka-dot rectangles 1/2" to the inside. Press.

2. Fold the same edge under 1" again and press. Topstitch 1/2" from the fold.

3. Pin one piece to the front matching raw edges, right sides facing. Pin the other piece to the other front edge. The folded edges should overlap in the middle.

4. Sew around all 4 sides.

5. Turn right side out and press.

6. Insert the pillow form.

Stitches in Rhyme

Modern Nursery

Peek-a-Boo Carrier Cover

Finished size: 32″ x 36″
Finished embroidered block size: 7″ x 7″
Designed and made by Amy

To protect a little one from the cold or from the sun, everyone needs a carrier cover. This sweet
pinwheel quilt goes from carrier cover to forever quilt by simply removing the straps.

Fabric and Supplies

Dark blue: fat quarter or 1/4 yard

Yellow polka dot: fat quarter or 1/4 yard

Yellow print: fat quarter or 1/4 yard

White polka dot: 1/4 yard

Solid white: 1/2 yard
(for embroidered square + quilt pieces)

Borders: 3/4 yard

Backing: 1 1/8 yards

Binding: 1/3 yard

Batting: 40"x40" piece plus 2- 1 1/2" x 10" scraps

Embroidery thread: DMC 312 or color of your choice

Fusible interfacing: 1/4 yard (20" wide)

Sew-on Velcro: 2 - 2" strips of 3/4" wide

Cutting Instructions

Dark blue: 4 - 4 1/2" squares (for corners),
4 - 4 7/8" squares (for half-square triangles),
and 2 - 5" x 10" strips (for straps)

Yellow polka dot: 4 - 4 7/8" squares
(for half square triangles)

Yellow print: 4 - 4 1/2" squares (for solid squares)

White polka dot: 8 - 4 7/8" squares
(for half square triangles)

Solid white: 8 - 4 7/8" squares (for half square triangles)
and 1 - 9" square for embroidery

Borders: 2 - 6 1/4" x 24 1/2" strips and
2 - 4 1/4" x 36 1/4" strips

Backing: 40" square

Batting: 40" square plus 1 - 1 1/2" x 10" scraps for straps

Binding: 4 - 2 1/2" x width of fabric strips
(or a total of 144")

Make the Center Block

Embroider the block of your choice following the Embroidery Instructions (page 14). Press on the reverse side. Trim to 7 1/2" square.

Half-Square Triangles

1. Place 1 - 4 7/8" square on top of another 4 7/8" square, right sides together. On the back of one square, draw a pencil line from one corner to the opposite corner.
2. Sew 1/4" from the line on each side.
3. Cut on the line to make 2 half-square triangles. Press the seam toward the darker of the 2 fabrics.
4. The square should measure 4 1/2". Make 8 yellow and white, 8 blue and polka dot, and 8 white and polka-dot blocks.

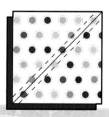

Assembly

Sew the blocks together following the Assembly Diagram.

Assembly Diagram

Borders

1. Sew a 6 1/2" x 24 1/2" border to each side.

2. Sew a 6 1/2" x 36 1/2" border to the top and bottom.

Finishing
Straps

1. Fold the short ends of a 5" x 10" blue rectangle 1/2" toward the reverse side and press.

2. Fold both long sides 1/4" to the reverse side and press.

3. Fold both long sides to the middle, overlapping until the strap measures 1 1/2" wide. Press and unfold.

4. Take a 1 1/2" x 10" piece of batting and place it along the middle of the reverse side of the blue rectangle from Step 1.

5. Fold sides over along the creases, with one side overlapping the other and encasing the batting.

6. Stitch along this center fold for the length of strap.

7. Repeat for the second strap.

8. Attach 2" lengths of Velcro tape at each end, one on the bottom side and one on the top side, so that when circling them around the carrier handle they stick together.

Loop side of
Velcro on outside

Hook side of
Velcro on inside

9. **Quilt and bind.** I quilted this on my home sewing machine using contrasting thread for both the top and bobbin threads. I stitched 1/4" from the block seams and around the center embroidered block. By using a contrasting thread in the bobbin, you get a nice repeat of the block pattern on the reverse side.

10. Pin the strap to the quilt on either side of embroidered square, matching the horizontal center of the strap to the seam between 2 blocks. Attach with 2 parallel lines of stitching through the center.

When your child outgrows the carrier, you can remove the straps and use this as a regular quilt.

Ready-Set-Go Diaper Bag

Finished size: 14″ deep x 18″ wide • Finished embroidered block size: 6″

Designed and made by Amy

Can we ever have enough bags? With pockets on the outside and pockets on the inside, this diaper bag holds everything you need with room to spare. You'll be using it long after the diaper phase is gone.

Fabric and Supplies

Stripe: 1 1/3 yard

Red polka dot: 1 yard

White: 1 – 9″ square

Orange: 1 fat quarter

Turquoise: 1 fat quarter

Yellow: 1 fat quarter

Green: 1 fat quarter

Fusible interfacing: 1/3 yard

Embroidery floss: DMC 704

Batting:

2 – 16″ x 22 1/2″ rectangles

2 – 6 1/2″ x 6 1/2″ (for outside pockets)

1 – 4 1/2″ x 46″ (for side panel)

2 – 2 x 19 1/2″ (for handles)

Optional:

2 – 8″ pieces of 3/8″ wide elastic

5″ pieces of ribbon for embellishment (must be wider than the elastic)

Cutting Instructions

White
1 – 9″ square for embroidery

Red Polka Dot
2 – 16″ x 22 1/2″ rectangles (for lining)

Stripe
2 – 3 1/2″ x 14 1/2″
2 – 5 1/2″ x 14 1/2″
1 – 2 1/2″ x 6 1/2″
1 – 3 1/2″ x 4 1/2″
1 – 3 1/2″ x 6 1/2″
1 – 4 1/2″ x 46″ (for side panel)
2 – 4 3/4″ x 19 1/2″ (for handles)

Orange
1 – 2″ x 10 1/2″
1 – 2 1/2″ x 4 1/2″

Turquoise
1 – 2 1/2″ x 4 1/2″
2 – 2 1/2″ x 6 1/2″
1 – 8 1/2″ x 14 1/2″

Yellow
1 – 2 1/2″ x 6 1/2″

Green
1 – 2 1/2″ x 4 1/2″
1 – 2″ x 10 1/2″

Contrasting Fabric for Pockets
1 – 6 1/2″ square for elastic top pocket
1 – 4 1/2″ x 6 1/2″ rectangle for slip pocket
2 – 8″ x 12″ rectangles for inside pockets using scraps from above

Interfacing:
1 – 9″ square for backing embroidery

This shows the bag inside – it's reversible!

Make the Center Block

Embroider the block of your choice following the Embroidery Instructions (page 14). Press on the reverse side.
Trim to 6 1/2" square.

Make the Front

Sew the pieces together in this order:

1. Stitch pieces 1, 2 and 3 together.

2. Stitch pieces 4 and 5 together.

3. Stitch these 2 sections together.

4. Stitch pieces 6 and 7 together.

5. Stitch pieces 8 and 9 together.

6. Stitch the 8-9 section to piece 10.

7. Stitch this section to the bottom of pieces 6-7 from Step 4.

8. Stitch pieces 11 and 12 together.

9. Stitch this section to side of the section created in Step 7.

10. Stitch this section to the bottom of the section made in Step 3.

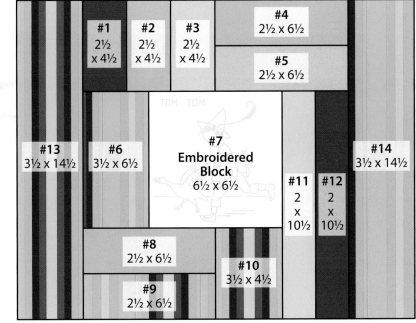

11. Stitch the remaining 3 1/2" x 14 1/2" striped pieces (13 and 14) to each end to complete the front of the bag.

The bag front should measure 18 1/2" x 14 1/2".

Layer the bag front with the batting and quilt as desired. I quilted this bag with parallel stitches about 1/2" apart.

Trim off excess batting after quilting each side.

Make the Back

1. Stitch a 5 1/2″ x 14 1/2″ striped rectangle to each side of the solid turquoise 8 1/2″ x 14 1/2″ rectangle.

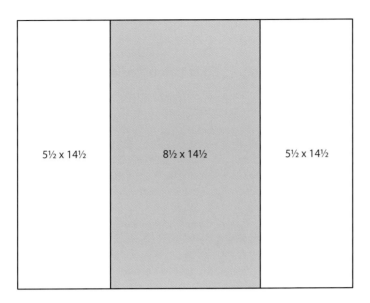

2. The bag back should measure 18 1/2″ x 14 1/2″ when pieced together.

3. Layer the bag back with the batting and quilt to match the front of the bag.

4. Using the corner template (below), cut curved bottom corners on front and back pieces.

**Bag front and back
Corner Template**

Make the Pockets

Note: Make the pockets and stitch them to the side panels BEFORE constructing the bag.

There are two options for pockets – one pocket style has elastic at the top edge and is gathered at the bottom edge to accommodate something larger, like a baby bottle. The other pocket style is one that lays flush with the body of the bag – a slip pocket.

Option 1: Elastic Top Pocket

1. Pin a 6 1/2" square of fabric to the same size batting. Quilt to match the bag.

2. Cut an 8" piece of 3/8" elastic. Zigzag stitch over the raw edge at the top of the pocket to keep it from fraying. Fold the top of the pocket - about 5/8" - toward the wrong side. Edge stitch to create a channel wide enough to accommodate the elastic.

Note: If you're adding ribbon trim to the top of the pocket, do it now. Just make sure you're leaving a channel wide enough for the elastic.

3. Attach a safety pin to one end of the elastic and run it through the channel. Pull the elastic until the pocket top fits the side panel (4 1/2"). With the ends of the elastic showing about 1/2" out of each side of the pocket, remove pin and stitch at each side of the pocket to hold elastic in place. Trim off the excess elastic. Fold the bottom edge 1/2" toward the wrong side and press. The pocket is now ready to pin to the side panel.

Option 2: Slip Pocket

1. Pin a 4 1/2" x 6 1/2" rectangle of fabric to the same size batting. Quilt to match the bag. Zigzag stitch over the raw edge at the top of the pocket to keep from fraying. Fold the top of the pocket toward the wrong side about 5/8".

Note: If you're adding ribbon trim to the top of the pocket, do it now.

2. Fold the bottom edge of the pocket 1/2" toward the wrong side and press. The pocket is now ready to pin to the side panel.

Make the Side Panels

1. Pin batting to the back of a 4 1/2" x 46" strip of fabric. Quilt to match the bag.

2. Mark 4" from the top of the bag. Place the top edge of the pocket at the 4" mark and pin. Baste the sides of each pocket to the side panels, within the seam allowance. Stitch the bottom of the pocket to the panel.

Note: For an elasticized pocket, sew a couple of pleats at the bottom edge of pocket, so it measures 4 1/2" to match the side panel.

3. Pin a panel to the front and back of the bag, right sides together, easing around the curved bottom corners. Stitch. Turn the bag right side out.

Make the Handles

1. Fold under 1/2" along one long edge of the 4 3/4" x 19 1/2" striped fabric; press.

2. Fold the same edge under 1" again; press.

3. Open the fold and place a 2" x 19" piece of batting along the 1" fold, lengthwise.

4. Fold long raw edge over batting.

5. Fold the pressed side over that.

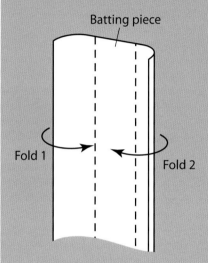

Batting piece

Fold 1   Fold 2

6. Pin in place.

7. Find the center of the panel and draw a vertical line from top to bottom at the center.

8. Stitch on the drawn center line and also 1/2" to both sides of center line.

9. Pin the finished handles to the right side of the top of the bag 3" in from the side seams, with the ends of the handles even with the raw edge of the top of the bag.

10. Baste in place.

Make the Lining

Pockets

1. Fold both side edges of the 8" x 12" pocket pieces 3/8" to the wrong side and press the folds. Fold in another 3/8" and press again. Repeat this process with the top and bottom edges. Topstitch along the top edge of the pocket. Center the pockets on the bag lining. With the pocket folds facing down, pin in place and stitch the sides and the bottom. If desired, stitch down the middle of the pocket to form a divider.

Front/Back

1. Pin 2 - 16" x 22 1/2" red polka-dot rectangles together, right sides facing. Sew the side and bottom edges, leaving a 6" opening at the bottom for turning. Press the seams open.

Shape Bag Bottom

1. To shape the bottom, create a flattened triangle in each bottom corner by matching the side seam to the bottom seam (right sides together). Measure 2" from the point of the triangle. Draw a line across the bottom at this point. The line should measure about 4". Stitch on the line. Trim the triangle 1/4" from the seam.

Lining Assembly

1. Place the bag body inside the bag lining, right sides together. The handles should be between the bag and the lining. Match the side seams and pin.

2. Stitch the bag to the lining around the top edge.

3. Turn the bag and lining right sides out through the 6" opening at the bottom.

4. Pull the lining out of the bag and whipstitch the 6" opening closed by hand. Push the lining back into the bag.

5. Press the top edge. Topstitch 1/4" from top edge of bag and again 1/4" down from that.

Magic Changing Pad

Finished size: 23″ x 35″ • 12″ square pocket pillow

Designed and made by Donna

This handy changing pad folds up into its own storage pocket, which can double as a pillow.
The inside pocket is large enough to hold a few diapers and a package of wipes.
The soft flannel feels so good on baby's tender skin and provides needed padding and protection.

Fabric and Supplies

Polka dot flannel: 2 yards

Red: 1 fat quarter (inside pocket)

Yellow: 1 fat quarter (inside pocket)

Blue: 1 fat quarter (inside pocket)

White: 14″ square for embroidery

Fusible interfacing:1/2 yard for embroidery backing

Non-fusible interfacing: 1/2 yard

Embroidery floss

Crayola crayons
(optional; see Embroidery Instructions, page 14)

Batting: 1 yard or 1 – 26″ x 38″ scrap of thin batting
(preferably fusible)

Freezer paper

Cutting Instructions

White or muslin: 1 – 14″ square of white

Fusible interfacing: 1 – 14″ square

Non-fusible interfacing
1 – 14″ square
1 – 8″ circle (template A on page 43)
1 – 10″ x 13″ oval (template B on page 43)

Polka-Dot Flannel
1 – 12 1/2″ square for pocket
2 – 26″ x 38″ rectangles for bag
12″ circle for optional pocket yo-yo
(template C on page 43)

Red: 1 – 12 1/2″ square for pocket front

Yellow: 1 – 8″ circle (template A)

Blue: 1 – 10″ x 13″ oval (template B)

Batting: 1 – 26″ x 38

1 - 3/4″ Velcro dot

Construction

1. Embroider the block of your choice according to the Embroidery Instructions (page 14).

2. Press the square on the reverse side.

Make the Front Pocket

1. Trace quarter circle template A onto freezer paper and cut out slightly outside the line.

2. Fold the front red square into fourths (in half and then in half again). Press the freezer paper pattern to the fabric, matching the right angle with the folded corner.

3. Cut the circle out, being careful to cut exactly on the line.

4. Take the 14" red square with the circle cut out of the middle and place it face down (right sides together) on top of the 14" interfacing square.

5. Sew around the inside edge of the circle, using a 1/4" seam.

6. Trim the stabilizer away along the edge of the circle opening. Clip the inside circle about every 1/2", being careful not to cut through the stitching.

7. Turn the block right side out through the opening in the stabilizer and press flat to create the frame. Rolling the seam edge back and forth in your fingers will help smooth out the edge and create a frame with a nice round circle opening.

8. Place the frame on top of the embroidered square with the embroidered design centered in the circle opening. Pin in place. Refer to the photo on page 42.

9. Edge stitch around the opening through all layers. Stitch again 1/8" from the first stitches so that you have a double row of stitching around the center circle.

10. Trim to 12 1/2" square.

11. Fold one edge of the 12 1/2" square polka-dot flannel to the reverse side 1/2" and press. Stitch along this side 3/8" from the fold.

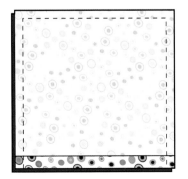

12. Place this square face down on the framed square with the folded edge at the bottom. Sew a 1/4" seam on 3 sides, leaving the folded edge side open.

13. Trim the corners and turn right sides out. Press and set aside. The pocket should measure 12" from side to side.

Make the Changing Pad

1. Make a sandwich of the 2 main polka-dot flannel rectangles and the batting.

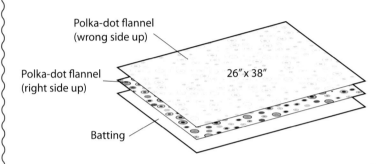

Polka-dot flannel (wrong side up)

Polka-dot flannel (right side up)

26" x 38"

Batting

2. Measure 6" from the top on both sides and mark with pin or marker. Measure 6" in from each corner on the top and mark. Draw a line from the top mark to the side mark on both edges. Cut along the drawn line through all 3 layers.

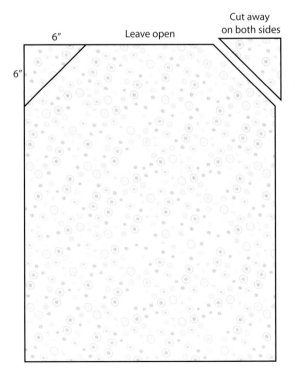

6"   Leave open   Cut away on both sides

6"

3. Using a 1/4″ seam, sew around all edges except the center top.

4. Trim the corners and turn right sides out. Press.

5. On the inside, measure 6″ from each side along the bottom edge and mark.

6. Draw a line from the top seam to the bottom mark on each side. Sew along these lines. These lines will aid in folding the quilt and serve as guides for further quilting.

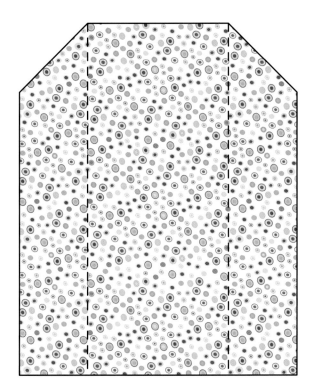

If you wish to quilt your pad, do so at this time. I drew a line every 6″ or so, both horizontally and vertically, and stitched along these lines to create a simple block quilting design.

7. Attach the pocket to the opening at the top by placing the reverse side of the pocket to the outer side of the pad, matching the open edges. Sew with a 1/2″ seam, catching only the pocket, batting and outer layer of the pad. Press the seam toward the pad.

8. Fold the inner top edge of the pad 1/2″ to the inside and whipstitch along the edge, encasing the seams.

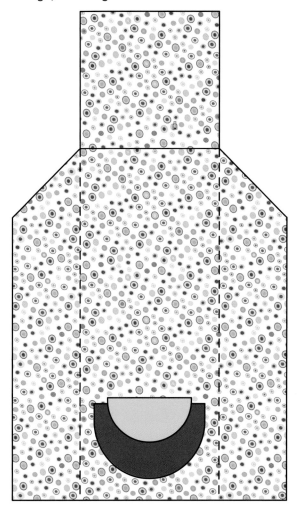

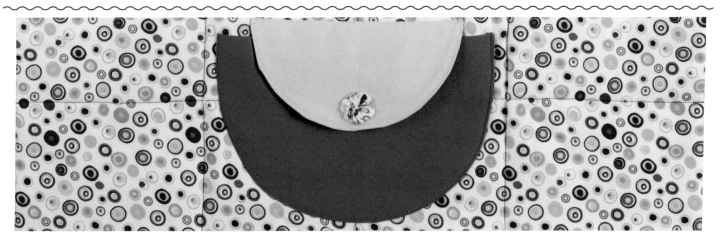

Make the Inside Pocket

1. Fuse the 8″ circle of interfacing to the 8″ yellow circle. Repeat with the 10″ x 13″ oval interfacing and blue fabric.

2. Fold the circle and oval in half, right sides together. Stitch, leaving about a 2″ opening for turning. Clip the seam every 1/2″ to help create a smooth curved edge.

3. Press the fabric at the opening to the inside along the seam line. This makes it easy to sew closed after turning.

4. Turn right sides out and press.

5. Place the large pocket (oval template B) on the inside of the pad, 2″ from the bottom and centered from side to side.

6. Sew in place by stitching just inside the curved edge. This will also close the space left open for turning. (These stitches will show on the outside of the pad, so I used white bobbin thread.)

7. Take the folded yellow circle (pocket flap) and edge stitch along the curved edge.

8. Place the pocket flap on top of the pocket. The top edge should be 1/2″ above the top edge of the pocket and centered from side to side. Attach to the pad by edge stitching along the top of the pocket flap.

9. Hand-stitch a Velcro circle to the blue pocket and to the inside of the yellow pocket flap.

10. If you wish to embellish your pocket with a yo-yo, start with a 2″ circle (template C on next page). Turn under and baste a 1/4″ seam all around the yo-yo circle using 2 strands of thread or 1 strand of heavy-duty thread such as buttonhole thread. Do not cut the thread.

11. Tug on the thread to form the yo-yo, tucking the turned hem into the center. Knot and/or take a couple stitches to fix the yo-yo. Stitch the yo-yo to the pocket flap.

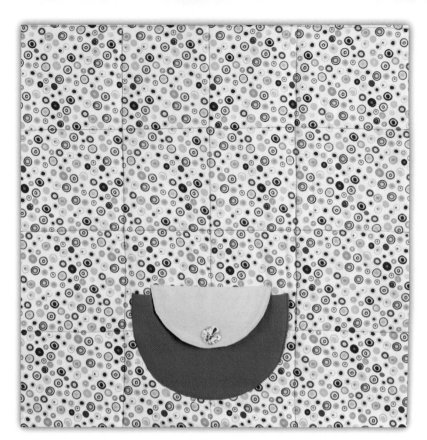

Fold and Store

Fold the sides of the pad inward along those first long stitched lines. Fold the bottom up about 10″. Fold again and again, tucking the pad inside the pillow/pocket on the last fold.

Stitches in Rhyme

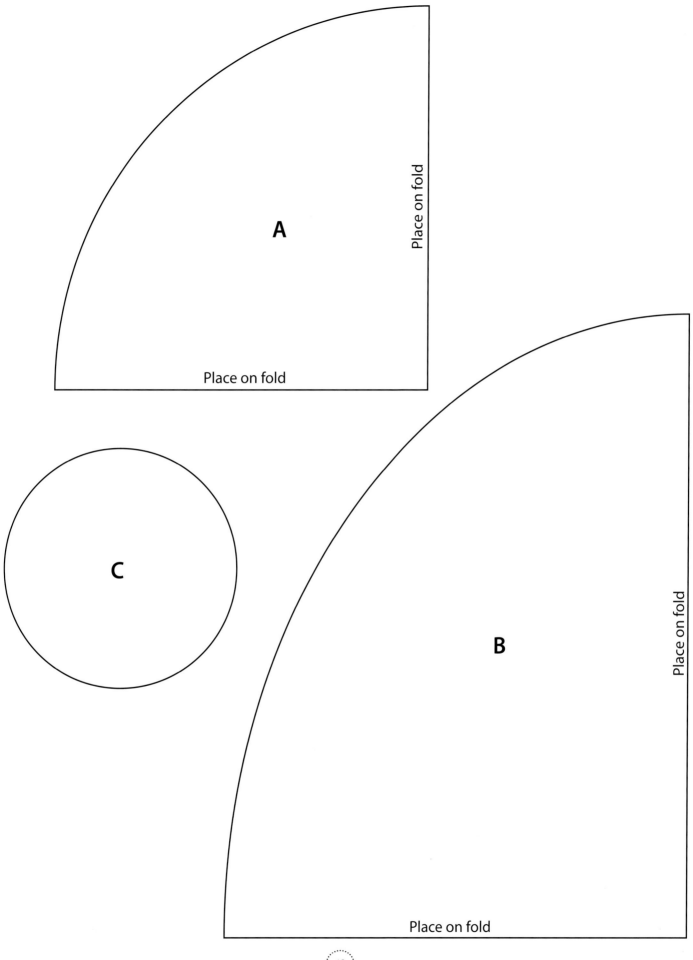

A

Place on fold

Place on fold

C

B

Place on fold

Place on fold

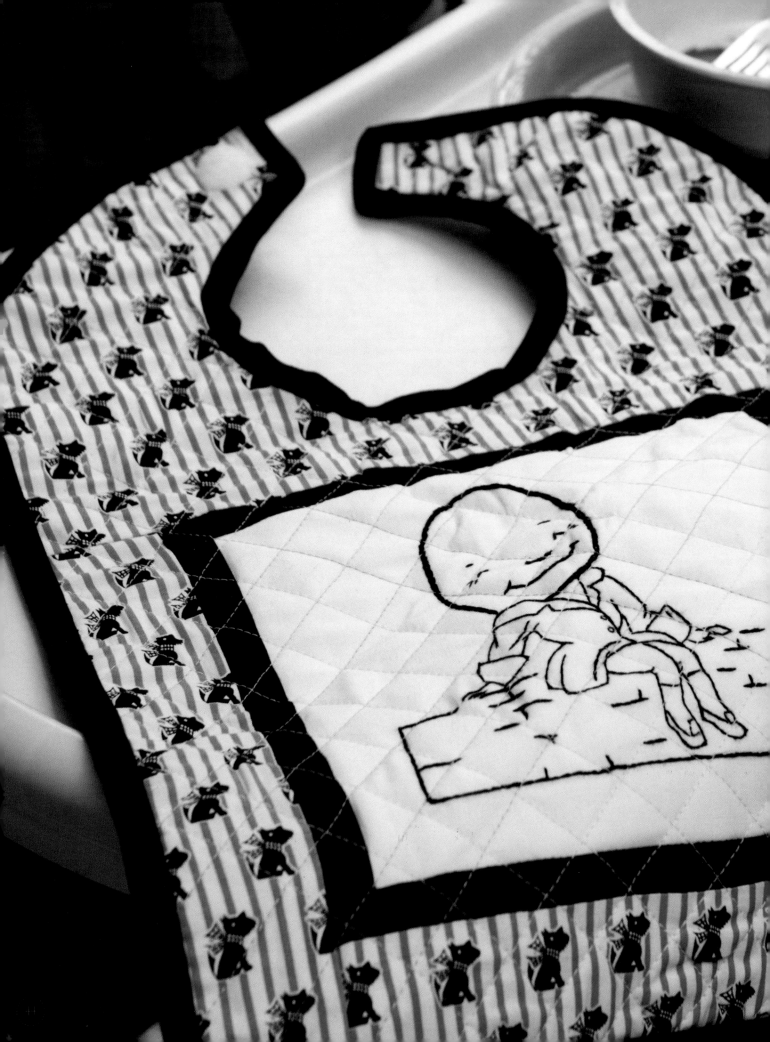

Humpty Dumpty Bib

Finished size: 11 1/2″ wide x 17 1/2″ long

Designed and made by Donna

Humpty Dumpty sits proudly on his wall, waiting for those inevitable crumbs, spills, and drools. This bib is made in much the same way as a large quilt – pieced, quilted, and bound – but it is small enough to finish in just one day. Practice your quilting skills and complete this bib for a special little someone.

Fabric and Supplies

White solid: 9″ square for embroidery

Fusible interfacing: 9″ square for back of embroidery

Embroidery floss: DMC 310

Print/stripe: 1 fat quarter for bib front

Solid: 1 fat quarter for bib back

Black: 1/4 yard for sashing and binding

Batting (low loft): 13″ x 18″ scrap

Velcro: 1 3/4″ dot – or – large snap

Freezer paper

Cutting Instructions

Print/Stripe

1 – 2″ x 8 1/2″ rectangle for bottom of bib
2 – 2″ x 10″ rectangles for sides of bib
1 – 8″ x 11 1/2″ rectangle for top of bib

Tip: If you choose a directional print, as I did, make sure the pattern is going in the right direction each time you cut or sew.

Black

2 – 1″ x 7 1/2″ strips
2 – 1″ x 8 1/2″ strips
2 – 2 1/4″ x width of fabric strips for binding

Backing: 13″ x 18″ rectangle

Fusible interfacing: 13″ x 18″ rectangle

Batting: 1 – 13″ x 18″ rectangle

Assembly

Embroider Humpty Dumpty or the design of your choice on a 9″ white square following the Embroidery Instructions (page 14). Trim block to 7 1/2″ square, making sure the embroidery is centered on the block.

1. Sew a 1″ x 7 1/2″ black strip to 2 opposite sides of the block.

2. Sew a 1″ x 8 1/2″ black strip to the top and bottom of the block.

3. Sew the 2″ x 8 1/2″ print/stripe rectangle to the bottom of the block.

4. Sew a 2″ x 10 1/2″ print/stripe rectangle to the 2 opposite sides of the block.

5. Trace the bib top template (page 90) onto freezer paper. Fold the freezer paper on the fold line and cut out on the drawn line, including the neck opening.

6. Lay the freezer paper template on the 8″ x 11 1/2″ print/stripe rectangle. Trace around the neck opening and outer edge onto the right side of the print/stripe rectangle. This can be done with a permanent pen as it will not show; you don't want the lines to disappear before you are ready to cut. Mark the center of the top of the neck opening for cutting later. Remove the freezer paper.

7. Sew the marked 8″ x 11 1/2″ print piece to the top of the bib, right sides facing, making sure the embroidered block is right side up. Your bib should measure about 11 1/2″ wide and 18 1/2″ long.

8. Layer the backing fabric (right side down), batting and bib (right side up). Center the bib on the backing and padding. There should be about 1″ of backing and batting on each side and the top and bottom. Pin every 2″ or so, just as you would if you were quilting a larger quilt.

Quilting

1. Begin by marking a diagonal line across the middle of the embroidered block, extending the lines to the edges in both directions. Stitch on the marked lines to stabilize the layers. I quilted a 3/4″ grid diagonally in both directions. Quilt right across the neck opening all the way to the edges. Remove the pins as you sew. Press when you are finished quilting.

2. Square and trim the bib along the bottom and sides. Cut along the traced lines on the back of the bib for the top of the bib. Cut from the outer edge to the neck opening at the marked center, and cut out the neck opening.

Finishing

1. You need 68″ total for the binding. Fold the strip in half lengthwise, wrong sides together, and press. Attach the binding to the front of the bib, starting on a side. Miter the square corners as you would any quilt binding and ease the binding around the curved edges and neck opening. Turn the binding to the back and stitch in place.

2. Sew the Velcro dot or a large snap to the neck opening and you are done. Snack time!

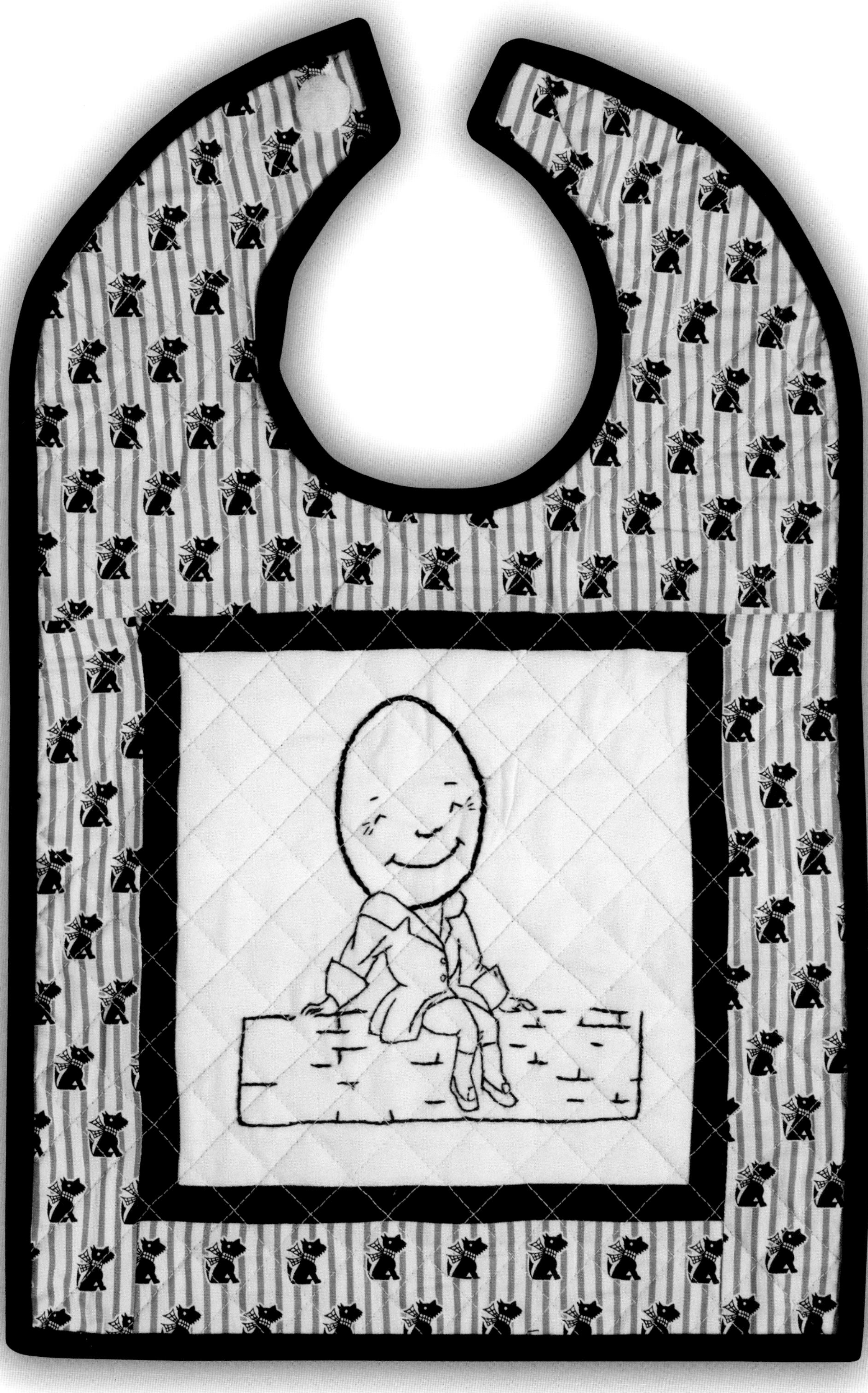

Storytime Scrapbook Cover

Fits standard scrapbook for 12″ x 12″ pages
Designed and made by Donna

My mother kept scrapbooks all of her adult life. She kept one for herself, one for my brother and one for me. Those scrapbooks are a wealth of information on life from the 1930s through the 1990s. They also have made researching family history much easier. Whether you are an avid scrapbooker or starting your first scrapbook, it is nice to have a cover to protect and enhance the memories.

Note: This cover is designed for a standard scrapbook that holds 12" x 12" pages. If your book is a different size, adjust the pattern and materials accordingly. The cover is adjustable to expand as you add more pages to the scrapbook. It also has a pocket in the back for an ID card or special keepsakes.

Fabric and Supplies

Red stripe: 1/2 yard

Lining: 1/2 yard

Solid white: 2 – 9 1/2" squares (1 for embroidered block and 1 for backing the block)

Interfacing: 1 – 9 1/2" square for backing the embroidery

Red solid: scraps (or fat quarter - 4 – 1" x 8" pieces) for flange

White tone-on-tone border: 1 fat quarter

Ribbon or rickrack trim: 1 yard 1/4" wide

Batting: 1 – 9 1/2" " square piece (preferably fusible batting)

Embroidery floss: DMC 321

Before You Cut

Open your scrapbook out flat and measure the height and width. Mine measured 12 1/2" high x 27 3/4" long. If your scrapbook is a different size, add 1/2" to the cover and lining height and a minimum of 10" to the width. I cut mine longer than this to allow for the addition of lots of pages.

Cutting Instructions

Red Stripe
1 – 13 1/2" x 41 1/2" for the cover
2 – 13 1/2" x 2 1/2" strips for the back straps
1 – 4" x 9" rectangle for the pocket

Lining: 1 – 13 1/2" x 41 1/2"

Solid white: 2 – 9 1/2" squares

Interfacing: 1 – 9 1/2" square for backing the embroidery

Red solid: 4 – 1" x 7 1/2"

White-on-White print
2 – 1 1/2" x 8"
2 – 1 1/2" x 9 1/2"

Ribbon or rick rack trim : 4 – 8 1/4" pieces

Embroidered Block

1. Embroider the block of your choice following the Embroidery Instructions (page 14).

2. Trim the block to 7 1/2" square, being sure to center the embroidery.

3. Fold the 1" red flange strips in half the long way, right side out, and press.

4. Align the raw edge of the block with the raw edges of the folded strip and baste in place. Sew the 2 sides first, then the top and bottom.

5. Sew a 1 1/2" x 7 1/2" white border strip to 2 opposite sides. Then sew a 1 1/2" x 9 1/2" white border strip to the top and bottom. Be very careful to sew an accurate scant 1/4" seam. You want the red folded border to show evenly all the way around the block.

6. Layer the batting, embroidered block and block lining together. The batting should be on the bottom, then the block (face up), then the lining (face down). Sew around all 4 sides using a 1/4" seam. Trim the corners for turning.

7. Cut a slit near the middle of the lining that is about 3" long. Be extremely careful to not cut the embroidered block. Turn the block right side out through the slit. Press.

8. If you want to quilt the block, do so now. I did a single line of stitches to outline the Mother Goose design and left the rest of the block unquilted.

Make the Cover

1. Lay the red stripe and lining together, right sides facing. Sew around the outer edge using a scant 1/4" seam. Leave a 3" - 4" opening on one short end for turning. Trim the corners and turn the cover right side out. Whip stitch the opening closed. Press.

2. Lay the cover face down on your work surface with the lining facing up. Fold the left end 3 1/2" toward the lining. Pin or baste the top and bottom edges to temporarily hold them together. Press the cover along the fold, making sure to press a good sharp crease. This will be the front edge of the cover.

3. Slide the front edge over the front of the scrapbook. Wrap the cover around and tuck it into the back so the cover is smooth and tight.

4. Center the embroidered block on the front of the scrapbook cover. Pin in place. Remove the cover from the scrapbook. Remove the basting stitches or pins from the edges and open the cover.

Attach the Block and Trim

Note: I purchased adhesive-backed ribbon in the scrapbooking department of my local shop. The adhesive made it easy to position the ribbon and sew it down without needing to pin it. If you use regular ribbon or rick rack, secure it in place with a dab of fabric glue before sewing. Pinning the trim in place and removing the pins as you sew may cause it to slip, so I recommend using glue.

1. With the block still pinned to the cover, lay 2 pieces of the trim on opposite sides of the block, centering the trim on the white border. If the trim isn't adhesive backed, use a couple dabs of glue to hold it in place.

2. Lay the remaining 2 pieces of trim on the top and bottom of the block, again securing it to the center of the white border. The ends of the top and bottom trim should slightly overlap the side pieces.

3. Sew the trim to the block and cover (sew through all layers). If using ribbon, first sew along the outer edge, then sew along the inner edge. If using rick rack, stitch down the middle. You are sewing through several layers, so sew slowly, using a medium length stitch and a sharp needle.

Finish the Cover

1. Turn the left front side of the cover 3 1/2" toward the inside along the ironed crease and whip stitch the top and bottom edges together.

2. To make the back strap, lay the 2 – 2 1/2" x 13 1/2" red stripe strips together, right sides facing. Sew around all 4 sides using a 1/4" seam and leaving about a 2" opening on one long side for turning. Clip the corners and turn right side out. Press.

3. Edge stitch all the way around the strip. This will close the opening and strengthen the strap all in one step.

4. Open the cover so the lining is facing up. Pin the strap to the right hand end. Attach the strap with a whipstitch along the top and bottom.

Sew strap to end at top and bottom

Make the Pocket

1. Fold the 4" x 9" pocket rectangle in half the long way. Sew along the 3 raw edges, leaving a 2" opening for turning. Clip the corners and turn right side out. Press.

2. Sew the pocket to the back of the cover, about 3" from the end and 2" - 3" from the bottom.

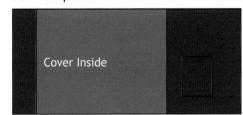

Cover Inside

3. Slip the front of the cover over the front of the scrapbook. Wrap the cover around to the back and slide the back of the scrapbook between the strap and the cover. Pull the cover toward the center of the scrapbook until it fits snugly.

4. Slip a note card in the pocket and start filling those pages.

Windmill Block Toy

Finished size: 7″ x 7″ cube

Designed and made by Amy

Safe for all ages, this giant block can be completed in no time
and makes a perfect gift. Why not make several?

Fabric and Supplies

Blue print: 1/4 yard

Red print: 1/4 yard

Red polka dot: 1/8 yard

Solid white: 1/4 yard

All-purpose woven fusible interfacing: 1/4 yard

Embroidery floss: DMC 321, 310

Polyfill stuffing: 1 – 12 oz. bag

Cutting Instructions

White: 2 – 9" squares for embroidery

Blue: 2 – 2 1/4" x 23"

Red print: 2 – 2 1/4" x 23"

Red polka dot: 1 – 2 1/4" x 23"

Interfacing or stabilizer: 2 – 9" squares for backing the embroidery

Windmill Blocks

Embroider 2 blocks of your choice following the Embroidery Instructions on page 14. Trim to 7 1/2" square.

Note: It's not necessary for the same material to be used in each square. 2 1/2" x 5 3/4" scraps can be used in place of making strip sets. However, each set requires a strip of one coordinating fabric to make the windmill pattern work.

1. Make a red print/blue print/red polka-dot strip set using 3 - 2 1/4" x 23" strips sewn together along the long side.

2. Press seams to one side.

3. Make a second strip set that is red print/white/blue print. Press seams to one side.

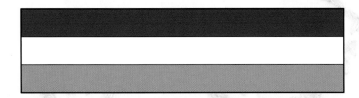

4. Subcut each strip into 4 – 5 3/4" squares.

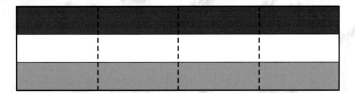

5. Place a mark in the corners indicated by A.

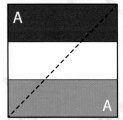

6. Cut each square in half diagonally. You must cut each square in the same direction to create 2 squares - one with red at the center and one with blue at the center.

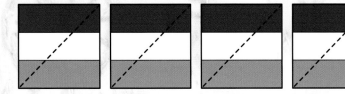

Stitches in Rhyme

7. Join triangles by placing the A corners in the center, forming a windmill pattern.

8. Repeat, rearranging the strips as desired.

   You should now have 4 completed windmill blocks for 4 sides of the cube. Trim each windmill block to 7 1/2" square.

9. Join 4 windmill blocks into a row.

10. Sew the ends of the row together (right sides facing) to make a continuous loop.

11. Sew one embroidered square to the loop to form the top of the cube.

12. Sew the other embroidered square to form the bottom of the cube, leaving a 3" opening to turn the cube right side out and for stuffing. Fill the cube with stuffing, using the handle of a wooden spoon to force the stuffing into the corners. When it's filled to your satisfaction, whipstitch the opening closed.

Humpty Dumpty and Friends

Finished size: about 10″ plus arms and legs

Designed by Donna; made by Jackie Rudolph

Humpty Dumpty and his friends are all good eggs. And just like real eggs, they can be any color you want them to be. Use hand-dyed or tea-stained fabric to give them a vintage look.

Warning: These guys are like eating potato chips. You can't stop at just one!

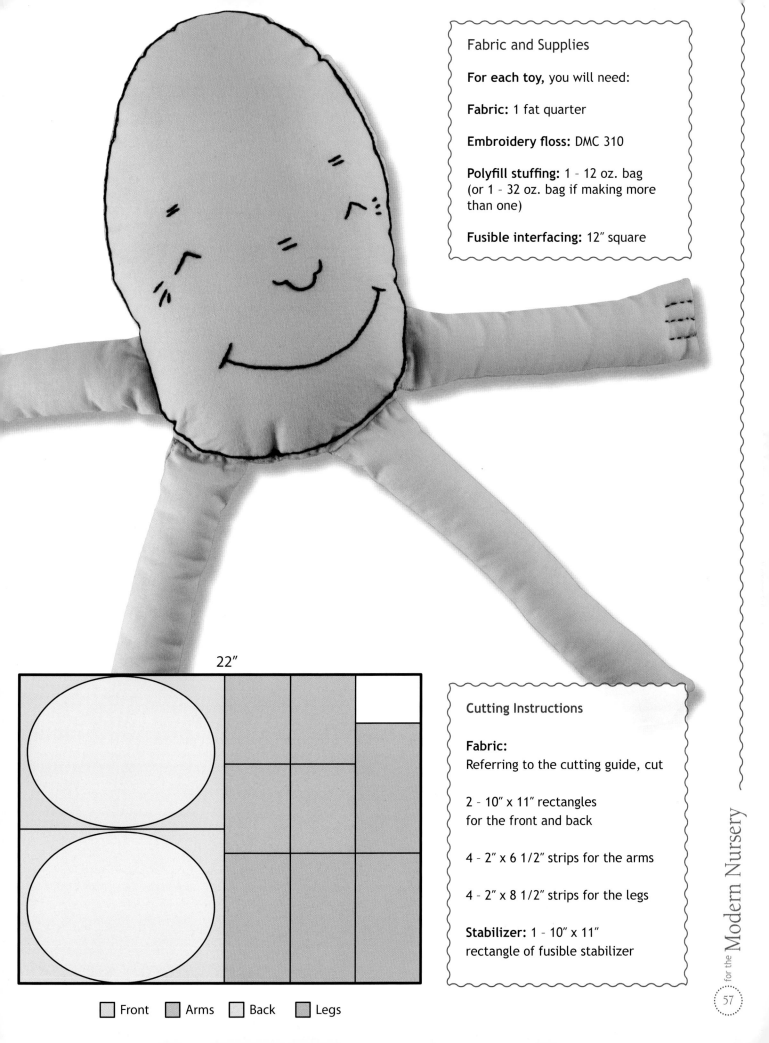

22″

Cutting Instructions

Fabric:
Referring to the cutting guide, cut

2 – 10″ x 11″ rectangles
for the front and back

4 – 2″ x 6 1/2″ strips for the arms

4 – 2″ x 8 1/2″ strips for the legs

Stabilizer: 1 – 10″ x 11″
rectangle of fusible stabilizer

☐ Front ☐ Arms ☐ Back ☐ Legs

Embroidery

See Embroidery Instructions on page 14.

1. Trace the face pattern and cutting lines from the templates (pages 91-92) onto the right side of one 10" x 11" rectangle. Place a mark or a notch at the top and bottom, as indicated on the pattern. This will be the front.

2. Trace the outside cutting line, top and bottom marks, and marks for the arms and legs on the reverse (back) side of the second 10" x 11" rectangle. This is the back.

4. Iron the stabilizer to the reverse side of the front.

5. Embroider the design on the front. I used a stem stitch and 2 strands of embroidery floss. Press on the reverse side when finished.

6. Cut out the front and back ovals on the traced line.

Assembly

1. Sew 2 – 6 1/2" strips together, wrong sides facing, for each arm and 2 – 8 1/2" strips for each leg, using a 1/4" seam. Leave one short end open for turning and backstitch at the beginning and end. Turn right side out.

2. If you want to make fingers, it is easier to do this before completely stuffing the arms. Push a bit of stuffing all the way down to the end of each arm. Use enough stuffing to make them plump, but not so much that you can't sew through it easily. Machine or hand-stitch the fingers.

3. Finish stuffing the arms and stuff the legs to the desired firmness, leaving about 1/2" unstuffed at the open end. Baste or pin the open end closed.

4. Pin the arms and legs in place on the back oval. The raw edges of the arms and legs should line up with the raw edge of the oval, with the arms and legs to the inside.

5. Place the front face down on the back and limbs, matching the top and bottom marks.

6. Sew together using a 1/2" seam; leave a 3" opening on one side for turning and stuffing. Backstitch at the beginning and end of the seam, and make sure you securely stitch the arms and legs as you sew. You may even want to stitch forward and reverse over the arms and legs to make sure they won't pull out. It gets a bit crowded inside, so go slow when you sew everything together.

7. Turn right side out. You can use the arms or legs to help with this, but pull gently.

8. Stuff to the desired firmness and whipstitch the opening closed.

Stitches in Rhyme

Momma Goose Hold-all

Finished size: 25″ from head to toe
Designed and made by Donna

The inspiration for this hold-all was a vintage clothespin bag. By opening up the "wings," it makes a fun bag for holding diapers, wipes, toys, laundry or even surprise presents. The "Mother Goose" fabric by Whistler Studios for Windham fabrics was perfect for the bag. This bag is not quilted, but you could certainly quilt it if you want.

Stitches in Rhyme

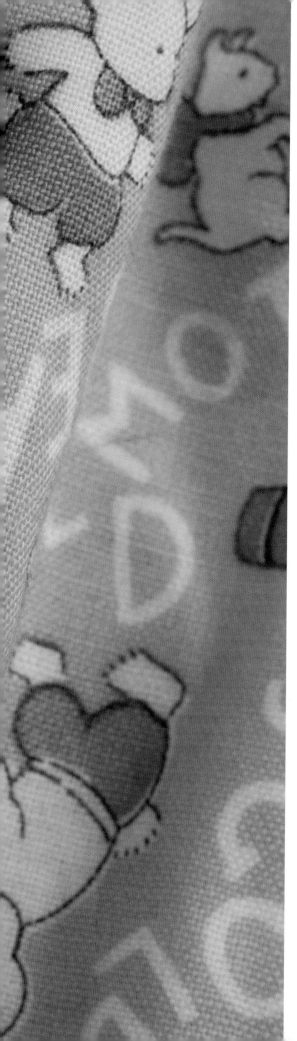

Fabric and Supplies

Mother Goose (outer) fabric:
1/2 yard or 2 fat quarters

Solid white: 1/2 yard (head and lining)

Orange: 1 fat eighth for feet and bill

Ribbon: 1 yard of 1/2" wide ribbon

1 - 3/8" or 1/2" black button (for the eye)

Thread to match the feet

Polyfill stuffing: 1 - 12 oz. bag for head and feet

3 - 1/2" buttons for front (optional)

Poster board or cardstock at least 14" x 20"
for making templates (optional - see Cutting
Instructions)

Glue or adhesive spray
(optional - see Cutting Instructions)

Pen or pencil for tracing pattern onto fabric

Cutting Instructions

1. Photocopy the patterns (pages 93-96). Be sure to copy them at 100%. Make 2 copies of the top and bottom sections – 1 for the front and 1 for the back.

2. Cut out each piece. Glue or tape the body pieces together where the pattern overlaps.

3. To make stiff templates, adhere the paper patterns to poster board or cardstock and cut out the pieces. This step is optional, but I found the stiff patterns much easier to work with than the paper patterns.

4. Fold the outer (Mother Goose) fabric in half to make a folded piece that is 9″ wide and the width of the fabric long (~42″). If using fat quarters, fold each piece in half to make 2 pieces 9″ wide x 22″ long.

5. Lay the front and back templates on the fold and trace the pattern onto the fabric. It doesn't matter if your fabric is folded right or wrong sides together, but sometimes it is easier to see the traced lines on the back of the fabric. The traced lines will not show on the finished bag.

6. Cut out 1 front and 1 back. Mark the pieces for easier assembly.

7. Repeat these steps for the white lining fabric.

8. Cut 2 head pieces from the remaining white fabric.

9. Cut 4 foot pieces and 2 bill pieces from the orange fabric.

Assembly

Feet

1. Place 2 foot pieces right sides together. Sew around the outer edge, leaving the top open. Turn right side out and press.

2. Stuff a small amount of stuffing into the feet. You want just enough to give them a bit of dimension.

3. Stitch the toes by machine or hand, using matching thread.

Body

1. Take 1 outer front and 1 lining front and place them right sides facing. Stitch around the top edge from the bottom of the curve on one side, up and across the top, then down to the bottom of the curve on the opposite side.

2. Clip the corners and curves. Turn right side out and press.

3. Repeat for the back, stitching from the bottom of the slant on one side, up and across the top, then down to the bottom of the slant on the opposite side. Turn right side out.

4. Pin the outer front to the outer back, right sides facing. Continue pinning the front lining to the back lining, matching the seams at the bottom of the curve with the seams at the bottom of the slant.

5. Stitch one long seam on both sides, leaving the bottom edges open.

6. Turn the bag so that the outer fabric is right sides together on the inside, and the lining is facing out.

7. Tuck the feet inside the bag and position them equal distance from each side seam, with the toes facing out, matching all raw edges. Sew a 1/2″ seam across the bottom of the bag.

8. Turn the bag right side out.

Stitches in Rhyme

Head

1. Place 1 head piece and 1 bill piece together as noted on the pattern, right sides facing. Stitch. Repeat using the other head and bill pieces. Press the seams open.

2. Place the 2 head sections together, right sides facing, matching the bill seams. Stitch around the head, leaving the bottom (neck) open. Clip the seam at the curve of the neck and around the tip of the bill. Be very careful not to clip into the stitching.

3. Turn right side out and press.

4. Stuff the head, beginning with the bill. Poke a wad of stuffing all the way to the end of the bill and pack it tightly.

   The handle of a wooden spoon is helpful in packing the bill and the head. You want to stuff it quite full so that the head is rounded.

5. Turn the bottom edge of the fabric 1/4″ to the inside and whipstitch the bottom closed.

Assembly

1. To make a casing for the ribbon, sew a line of stitches 1″ from the top edge across both the front and back of the bag. Sew another line of stitches 3/8″ from the top edge across both the front and back of the bag. Snip the threads of the side seams between the 2 rows of stitches.

2. Cut an 8″ piece of ribbon and set it aside.

3. Using a safety pin or ribbon threader, thread the remaining ribbon into the casing beginning at one side of the front. This is the side where the bow will be. Continue threading the ribbon through the casing on the back. Now take the ribbon and thread it through the front and back again, ending on the same side where you began. You now have a continuous loop through the casing and 2 ends of the ribbon on the same side. Pull the ends to gather the neck.

4. Slip the head into the neck opening with the bill toward the same side as the ribbon ends. The neck should extend 2″ - 3″ inside the bag.

5. Pull the ribbon to tightly gather the top around the neck. Hold the top gathered edge back and whip stitch or tack the bag to the neck. Tie the ribbon into a nice bow and trim the ends if you wish.

6. Stitch the button eye to the head.

7. Take the 8″ piece of ribbon and form a loop. Stitch the loop to the back of the head, approximately opposite the eye. This loop is for hanging the bag so make sure your stitches are sturdy.

8. Sew 3 buttons to the front of the bag if desired.

Stitches in Rhyme

Quilt Label

Always include a label on your quilt. Minimum information should include the name of the maker, their city and state and the date finished or presented. Include as much information as possible for future generations.

Software is available in shops and online for creating decorative labels. The simplest label is a piece of fabric on which the information is hand-written using a permanent pen, such as a Micron fine tip marker. The markers come in many colors if you wish to coordinate the label with the quilt.

You may also use your computer to type the information and print it onto specially-prepared fabric using an ink-jet printer. Your name and date can be written directly onto the quilt back and either left as is or embroidered over. The possibilities are endless.

Sew the fabric label onto the quilt, typically on the back of the quilt.

Here is a sample that you may use to create your label.

Nursery Rhyme Quilt

Made by _____ (your name)

_____ (address, city, state)

Especially for

_____ (recipient)

Presented on

_____ (date)

The Blocks

There were 21 blocks in the original Nursery Rhyme Storybook Quilt series. The blocks were to be "transferred with carbon paper" onto a 7" square. Cream or off-white percale, sateen, muslin or broadcloth was recommended for the blocks. One yard of 36"-wide material would yield all 21 - 7" blocks for the complete quilt.

The finished quilt was to be 56" wide x 63" long, less seam allowances. Four and one-half yards of 36" fabric was required to join the blocks (alternate solid blocks and borders) and for the back of the quilt and binding. The lettering on the blocks was to be outlined in black embroidery floss to tie the blocks together. Colors for embroidering the designs were given with each block.

The blocks are presented here in the same order as they were published in the Omaha World-Herald. All of the projects in this book may be made with the block or blocks of your choice, and the designs may be embroidered using one color of floss or many colors. Those decisions are all up to you.

Block #	Name	Date published
1	Mary Had a Little Lamb	Sept. 4, 1940
2	Little Boy Blue	Sept. 11, 1940
3	Mistress Mary	Sept. 18, 1940
4	Tom-Tom	Sept. 25, 1940
5	Humpty Dumpty	Oct. 2, 1940
6	Little Bo Peep	Oct. 9, 1940
7	Little Tommy Tucker	Oct. 16, 1940
8	Simple Simon	Oct. 23, 1940
9	Peter Peter	Oct. 30, 1940
10	Ride a Cock Horse	Nov. 6, 1940
11	Mother Goose	Nov. 13, 1940
12	Hickory Dickory	Nov. 20, 1940
13	Wee Willie Winkie	Nov. 27, 1940
14	Little Jack Horner	Dec. 4, 1940
15	Sing a Song of Sixpence	Dec. 11, 1940
16	Jack and Jill	Dec. 18, 1940
17	Nimble Jack	Dec. 25, 1940
18	Mother Hubbard	Jan. 1, 1941
19	Polly Put the Kettle On	Jan. 8, 1941
20	See Saw	Jan. 15, 1941
21	Miss Muffet	Jan. 22, 1941

About Mother Goose Rhymes

These classic rhymes have been read, told and sung to children for centuries. Mother Goose is the imaginary author of a collection of English fairy tales and nursery rhymes dating to the 1600s. Sometimes she is depicted as an elderly country woman in a tall hat and shawl. Sometimes she is a goose, usually wearing a bonnet. Published in many ways since 1650, it is a rare shelf of children's books that doesn't include one adaptation of these tales. Nursery rhymes never go out of style!

Humpty Dumpty Sits on a Brick Wall

Reposes on Fifth Block of Nursery Quilt

"Humpty Dumpty sat on wall," is the theme of the fifth block of the nursery quilt series of 21 blocks appearing weekly in The World-Herald.

The pattern is to be transferred with carbon paper onto a piece of neutral colored material, seven inches square.

Bright red embroidery floss may be used to outline the bricks forming the wall on which Humpty Dumpty sits. For the flowers growing on the wall, use deep lavender floss and green for the stems and leaves for contrast.

Humpty Dumpty's suit in deep blue or brown in outline stitch with contrasting lighter blue or orange yellow for the cuffs and revers of the coat. Use white floss in making the French knots for the buttons of the coat.

Lemon yellow embroidery floss is suggested for outlining Humpty Dumpty's head. The mouth may be outlined in bright red with cream color or yellow for the nose and hands and blue for the eyes. Black or brown floss may be used for the slippers with deep tan for the socks. Outline the name of the block "Humpty Dumpty" in black embroidery floss.

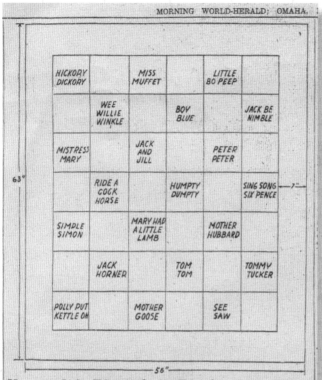

Samples of the original patterns from the Omaha World-Herald

MARY HAD A LITTLE LAMB

Block 1
Mary Had a Little Lamb

Mary had a little lamb,
Its fleece was white as snow;
And everywhere that Mary went
The lamb was sure to go.

Block 2
Little Boy Blue

Little boy blue come blow your horn
The sheep's in the meadow, the cow's in the corn;
But where is the boy who looks after the sheep
He's under a haycock fast asleep.

Block 3
Mistress Mary

Mistress Mary, quite contrary,
How does your garden grow?
With silver bells and cockle shells,
And pretty maids all in a row.

for the Modern Nursery

Block 4
Tom Tom

Tom, Tom, the piper's son,
Stole a pig and away did run;
The pig was eat, and Tom was beat,
And Tom went crying down the street.

Block 5
Humpty Dumpty

Humpty Dumpty sat on a wall,
Humpty Dumpty had a great fall.
All the king's horses,
And all the king's men,
Couldn't put Humpty together again.

LITTLE BO-PEEP

Block 6
Little Bo-Peep

Little Bo-Peep has lost her sheep,
And can't tell where to find them;
Leave them alone, and they'll come home,
Bringing their tails behind them.

Block 7
Tommy Tucker

Little Tommy Tucker sings for his supper;
What shall we give him? White bread and butter.
How shall he cut it, without e'er a knife?
How shall he marry, without e'er a wife?

for the Modern Nursery

Block 8
Simple Simon

Simple Simon met a pieman
Going to the fair;
Says Simple Simon to the pieman,
"Let me taste your ware."

Block 9
Peter Peter

Peter, Peter, pumpkin eater
Had a wife and couldn't keep her;
He put her in a pumpkin shell
And there he kept her very well.

for the Modern Nursery

Block 10
Ride a Cock Horse

Ride a cock-horse to Banbury Cross,
To see a fine lady upon a white horse;
With rings on her fingers and bells on her toes,
She shall have music wherever she goes.

MOTHER
GOOSE

Block 11
Mother Goose

Old Mother Goose
When she wanted to wander,
Would ride through the air
On a very fine gander.

Block 12
Hickory Dickory

Hickory, dickory, dock,
The mouse ran up the clock.
The clock struck one,
The mouse ran down,
Hickory, dickory, dock.

Block 13
Wee Willie Winkie

Wee Willie Winkie runs through the town,
Upstairs and downstairs in his nightgown,
Rapping at the window, crying through the lock,
"Are the children in their beds, for now it's eight o'clock?"

for the Modern Nursery

Block 14
Jack Horner

Little Jack Horner
Sat in the corner,
Eating a Christmas pie;
He put in his thumb,
And pulled out a plum,
And said, "What a good boy am I!"

Block 15
Sing a Song of Sixpence

Sing a song of sixpence,
A pocket full of rye;
Four and twenty blackbirds
Baked in a pie.

for the Modern Nursery

Block 16
Jack and Jill

Jack and Jill went up the hill
To fetch a pail of water;
Jack fell down and broke his crown
And Jill came tumbling after.

Block 17
Jack Be Nimble

Jack be nimble,
Jack be quick,
Jack jump over
The candle stick.

Block 18
Mother Hubbard

Old Mother Hubbard,
Went to the cupboard,
To get her poor dog a bone,
But when she got there
The cupboard was bare,
And so the poor dog had none.

POLLY - PUT
THE KETTLE ON

Block 19
Polly - Put the Kettle On

Polly put the kettle on,
Polly put the kettle on,
Polly put the kettle on,
We'll all have tea.

Block 20
See-Saw

See-Saw, Margery Daw,
Jacky shall have a new master;
Jacky shall earn but a penny a day,
Because he can't work any faster.

Block 21
Miss Muffet

Little Miss Muffet
Sat on a tuffet,
Eating her curds and whey;
There came a big spider,
Who sat down beside her
And frightened Miss Muffet away.

Humpty Dumpty

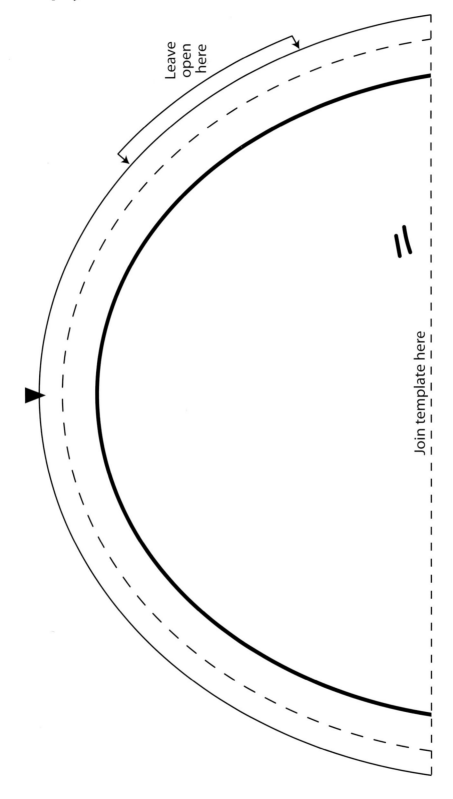

Leave open here

Join template here

Humpty Dumpty

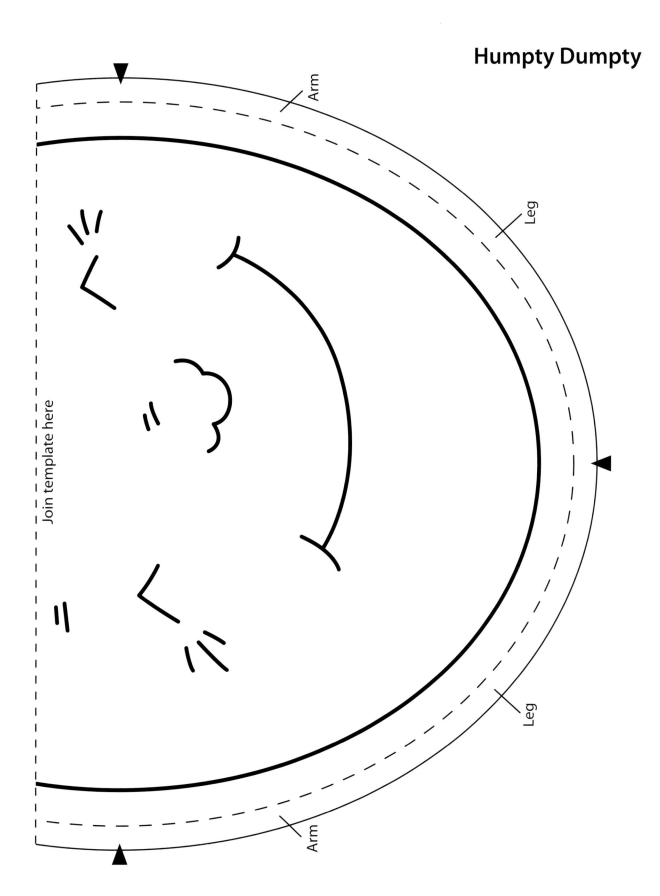

Arm

Leg

Join template here

Leg

Arm

Top

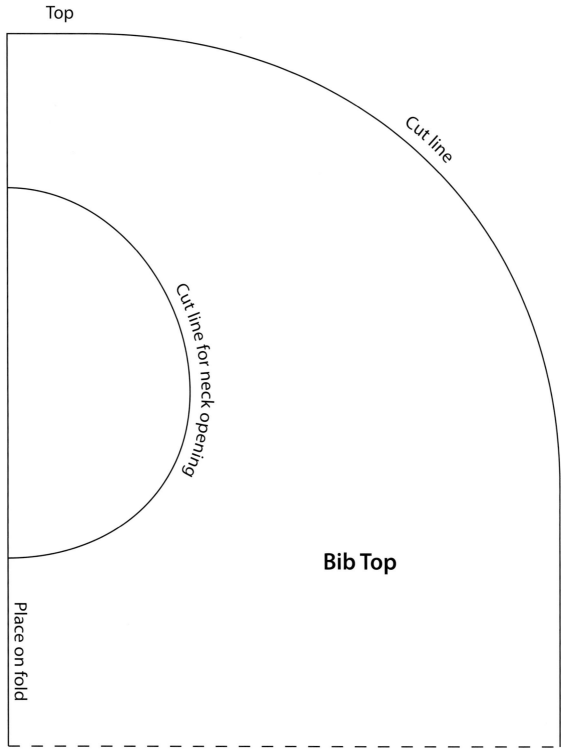

Cut line

Cut line for neck opening

Bib Top

Place on fold

Attach to block here

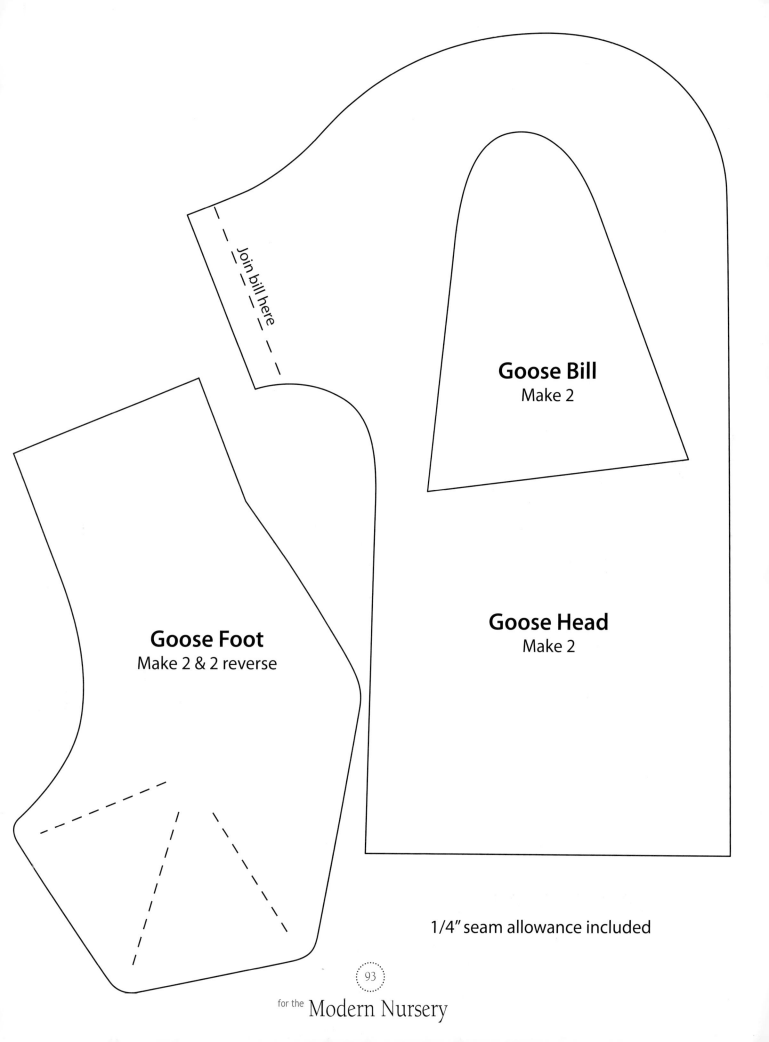

Join bill here

Goose Bill
Make 2

Goose Foot
Make 2 & 2 reverse

Goose Head
Make 2

1/4" seam allowance included

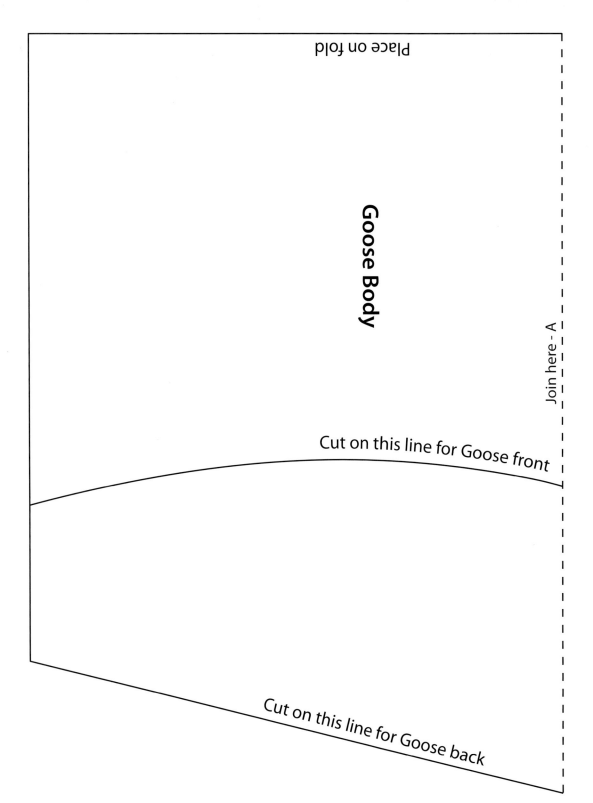

Place on fold

Goose Body

Join here - A

Cut on this line for Goose front

Cut on this line for Goose back

1/4" seam allowance included

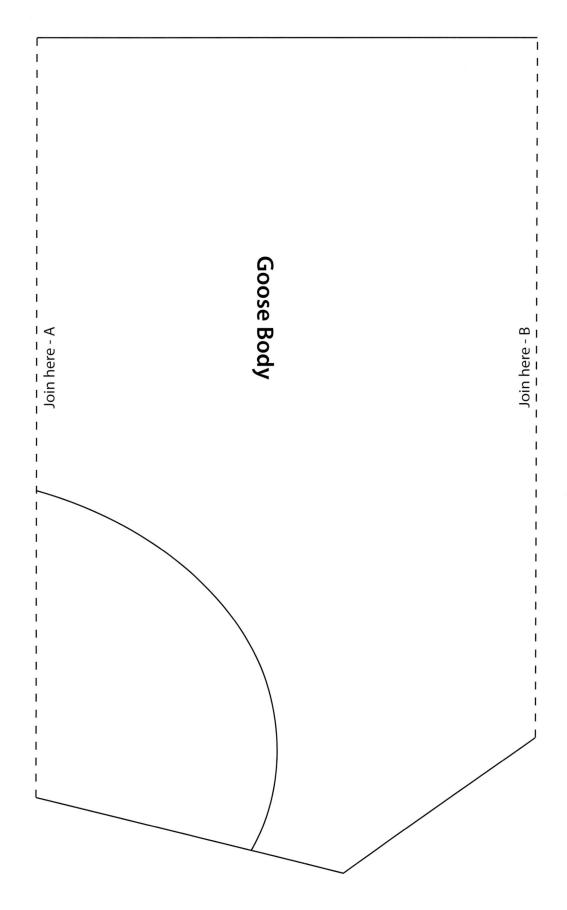

Join here - A

Goose Body

Join here - B

1/4" seam allowance included

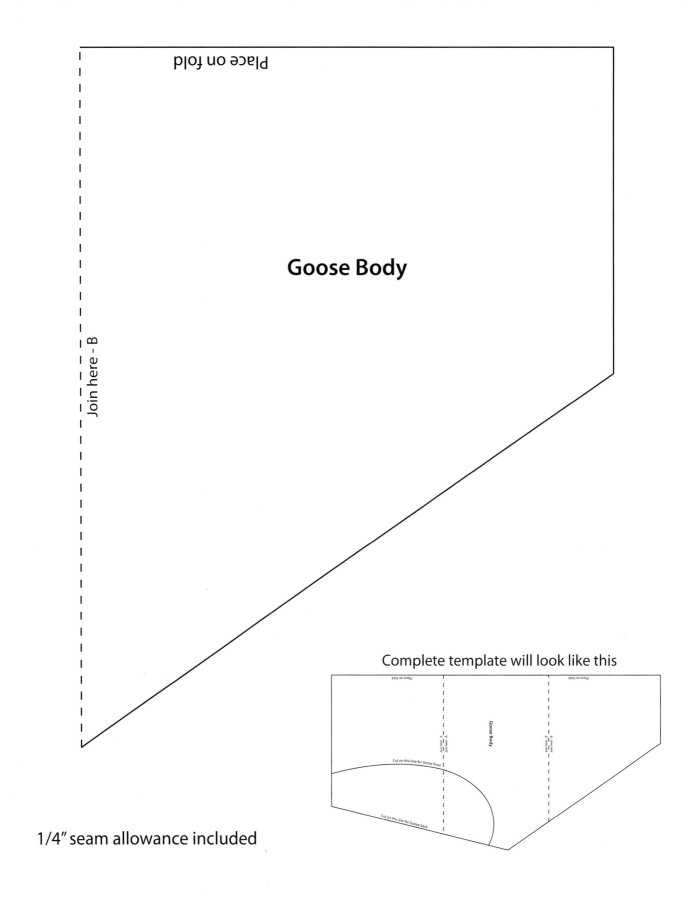

Place on fold

Goose Body

Join here - B

Complete template will look like this

1/4" seam allowance included